HOMO-SEXUAL PARTNER-SHIPS?

Why Same-Sex Relationships
Are Not a Christian Option

JOHN STOTT

INTERVARSITY PRESS
DOWNERS GROVE, ILLINOIS 60515

Published in the United States of America by InterVarsity Press, Downers Grove, Illinois; this material is adapted from chapter eight, "Homosexual Partnerships?" in Involvement: Social and Sexual Relationships in the Modern World, Volume II, published by Fleming H. Revell Company; used by permission.

InterVarsity Press is the book-publishing division of InterVarsity Christian Fellowship, a student movement active on campus at hundreds of universities, colleges and schools of nursing. For information about local and regional activities, write Public Relations Dept., InterVarsity Christian Fellowship, 6400 Schroeder Rd., P.O. Box 7895, Madison, WI 53707-7895.

Distributed in Canada through InterVarsity Press, 860 Denison St., Unit 3, Markham, Ontario L3R 4H1, Canada.

ISBN 0-8308-1102-8

Printed in the United States of America

Library of Congress Cataloging in Publication Data

Stott, John R. W.
      Homosexual partnerships?

      (Viewpoint Pamphlets)
      Adapted from v. 2, ch. 8, of the author's
Involvement, 1985.
      1. Homosexuality—Religious aspects—Christianity—
Controversial literature.   2. Homosexual couples.
I. Title.   II. Series: Viewpoint Pamphlets (Downers Grove, Ill.)
BR115.H6S76   1987   241'.66   87-3924
ISBN 0-8308-1102-8

15	14	13	12	11	10	9	8	7	6	5	4	3	2
98	97	96	95	94	93	92	91	90	89	88	87		

It is important to set the proper context for our discussion. Let me begin by affirming a number of truths that I will take for granted as I write.

First, *we are all human beings.* That is to say, there is no such phenomenon as "a homosexual." There are only people—human persons—made in the image and likeness of God, yet fallen. However strongly we may disapprove of homosexual practices, we have no liberty to dehumanize those who engage in them.

Second, *we are all sexual beings.* Our sexuality, according to both Scripture and experience, is basic to our humanness. When God made humankind, he made us male and female. So to talk about sex is to touch a point close to the center of our personality. The subject, therefore, demands an unusual degree of sensitivity because it involves our very identity.

Moreover, not only are we all sexual beings, but we all have a particular sexual orientation. Alfred C. Kinsey's famous investigation into human sexuality discovered that 4 per cent of men (at least of white American men) are exclusively homosexual throughout their lives and that as many as 37 per cent have some kind of homosexual experience between adolescence and old age. The percentage of homosexual women he found to be lower, although it rises to 4 per cent between the ages of 20 and 35.[1] The numbers are high enough to warrant Dr. Donald J. West's comment that "homosexuality is an extremely common condition."[2]

Third, *we are all sinners*. Indeed, we are all sexual sinners. The doctrine of total depravity asserts that every aspect of our humanity has been tainted and twisted by sin, including our sexuality. Merville Vincent comments, "In God's view I suspect we are all sexual deviants. I doubt if there is anyone who has not had a lustful thought that deviated from God's perfect ideal of sexuality."[3] Nobody (except Jesus) has been sexually sinless. There is no question, therefore, of coming to this study with a "holier-than-thou" attitude of moral superiority. We all stand under the judgment of God and are in urgent need of his grace. Besides, sexual sins are not the only sins, nor even necessarily the most sinful; pride and hypocrisy are surely worse.

Fourth, in addition to being human, sexual and sinful creatures, I take it that *we are all Christians*. The readers I have in mind are not people who reject the lordship of Jesus Christ, but rather those who earnestly desire to submit to it, believe that he exercises it through Scripture, and have a predisposition to follow God's will when it is known. Without this kind of commitment, it would be more difficult for us to find common ground. To be sure, God's standards for non-Christians are the same, but they are less ready to accept them.

Having set the context for our discussion, we are now ready to explore the issue: Are homosexual partnerships a Christian option? I phrase my question advisedly. It introduces us to three necessary distinctions.

First, we must distinguish between sins and crimes. According to God's law, adultery has always been a sin, but in most countries it is not an offense punishable by the state. Rape, by contrast, is both a sin and a crime. In Britain the Sexual Offenses Act of 1967 declared that a homosexual act performed between consenting adults over 21 in private should no longer be a criminal offense. "The Act did not in fact 'legalize' such behaviour," wrote Norman Anderson, "for it is still regarded by the law as immoral, and is devoid of any legal recognition; all the Act did was to remove the criminal sanction from such acts when performed in private between two consenting adults."[4]

Second, many distinguish between a homosexual orientation or "inversion" (for which people are not responsible) and homosexual physical practices (for which they are). The importance of this distinction goes beyond the attribution of responsibility to the attribution of guilt. We may not blame people for what they are, though we may for what they do. And in every discussion about homosexuality we must be rigorous in differentiating between this "being" and "doing"—that is, between a person's identity and activity, sexual preference and sexual practice, constitution and conduct.

But now we have to come to terms with a third distinction, namely, between homosexual practices which are casual (and probably anonymous) acts of self-gratification and those which (it is claimed) are just as expressive of authentic human love as is heterosexual intercourse in marriage. No responsible homosexual person (whether Christian or not) is advocating promiscuous "one night stands," let alone violence or the corruption of young people and children. What some are arguing, however—especially in the so-called Gay Christian Movement—is that a heterosexual marriage and a homosexual partnership are "two equally valid alternatives,"[5] being equally tender, mature and faithful.

The question before us, then, does not relate to homosexual practices of a casual nature, but whether homosexual partnerships—lifelong and loving—are a Christian option. Our concern is to subject prevailing views on the matter to biblical scrutiny. Is our sexual "preference" purely a matter of personal taste? Or has God revealed his will regarding a norm? In particular, can the Bible be shown to sanction homosexual partnerships, or at least not to condemn them?

The Biblical Prohibitions

The late Derrick Sherwin Bailey was the first Christian theologian to re-evaluate the traditional understanding of the biblical prohibitions. His famous book—of which all subsequent writers on this topic have had to take careful account—*Homosexuality and the Western Christian Tradition,* was published in 1955. Although many have not been able to accept his attempted reconstruction, other writers, less cautious in scholarly standards than he, regard his argument as merely preliminary and build on his foundations a much more permissive position. It is essential to consider this debate.

Four main biblical passages refer (or appear to refer) to the homosexual question negatively: (1) the story of Sodom (Gen 19:1-13) and the similar story of Gibeah (Judg 19); (2) the Levitical texts (Lev 18:22; 20:13) which prohibit "lying with a man as one lies with a woman"; (3) the apostle Paul's portrayal of decadent pagan society in his day (Rom 1:18-32); and (4) two Pauline lists of

sinners, each of which includes a reference to homosexual practices of some kind (1 Cor 6:9-10; 1 Tim 1:8-
11).

1. *The Stories of Sodom and Gibeah.* The Genesis nar-
rative makes it clear that "the men of Sodom were
wicked and were sinning greatly against the LORD"
(13:13) and that "the outcry against Sodom and Gomorrah" was "so great and their sin so grievous" that God
determined to investigate it (18:20-21), and in the end
"overthrew those cities and the entire plain, including
all those living in the cities" (19:25) by an act of judgment which was entirely consistent with the justice of
"the Judge of all the earth" (18:25). There is no contro-
versy about this background to the biblical story. The
question is: What was the sin of the people of Sodom
(and Gomorrah) which merited their obliteration?

The traditional Christian view has been that they
were guilty of homosexual practices, which they attempted (unsuccessfully) to inflict on the two angels whom
Lot was entertaining in his home—hence the word *sod-
omy.* But Sherwin Bailey challenged this interpretation
on two main grounds. First, it is a gratuitous assumption
(he argued) that the demand of the men of Sodom
"Bring them out to us, so that we may *know* them" meant
"so that we can have sex with them" (19:5 NIV). The
Hebrew word for "know" *(yada')* occurs 943 times in the
Old Testament, of which only ten occurrences refer to
physical intercourse, and even then only to heterosexual intercourse. It would therefore be better to translate
the phrase "so that we may get acquainted with them."
We can then understand the men's violence as due to
their anger that Lot had exceeded his rights as a resident alien, for he had welcomed two strangers into his
home "whose intentions might be hostile and whose

credentials . . . had not been examined."[6] In this case the sin of Sodom was to invade the privacy of Lot's home and flout the ancient rules of hospitality. Lot begged them to desist because, he said, the two men "have come under the protection of my roof" (v. 8).

Bailey's second argument was that the rest of the Old Testament nowhere suggests that the nature of Sodom's offense was homosexual. Instead, Isaiah implies that it was hypocrisy and social injustice (1:10-17); Jeremiah makes it adultery, deceit and general wickedness (23:14); and Ezekiel, arrogance, greed and indifference to the poor (16:49-50). Then Jesus himself (though Bailey does not mention this) on three separate occasions alluded to the inhabitants of Sodom and Gomorrah, declaring that it woud be "more bearable" for them on the day of judgment than for those who reject his gospel (Mt 10:15; 11:24; Lk 10:12). Yet in all these references there is not even a whiff or rumor of homosexual malpractice! It is only when we reach the Palestinian pseudepigraphical writings of the second century B.C. that Sodom's sin is identified as unnatural sexual behavior.[7] This finds a clear echo in the letter of Jude, in which it is said that "Sodom and Gomorrah and the surrounding towns gave themselves up to sexual immorality and perversion" (v. 7), and in the works of Philo and Josephus, Jewish writers who were shocked by the homosexual practices of Greek society.

Bailey handled the Gibeah story in the same way. Another resident alien (this time an anonymous "old man") invites two strangers (not angels but a Levite and his concubine) into his home. Evil men surround the house and make the same demand as the Sodomites, that the visitor be brought out "so that we may know him." The owner of the house first begs them not to be so "vile" to his "guest," and then offers his daughter and the concubine to them instead. The sin of the men of Gibeah, it is again suggested, was not their proposal of homosexual intercourse but their violation of the laws of hospitality.

But Bailey's case is not convincing for a number of reasons: (1) The adjectives "wicked," "vile" and "disgraceful" (Gen 19:7; Judg 19:23) do not seem appropriate to describe a breach of hospitality; (2) the offer of women instead "does look as if there is some sexual connotation to the episode"[8]; (3) although the verb *yada'* is used only ten times of sexual intercourse, six of these occurrences are in Genesis and one in the Sodom story itself (about Lot's daughters who had not "known" a man, v. 8); (4) for those of us who take the New Testament seriously, Jude's unequivocal statement cannot be dismissed as merely an error copied from Jewish pseudepigrapha. To be sure, homosexual behavior was not Sodom's only sin; but according to Scripture it was certainly one of them.

2. *The Leviticus Texts.* Both texts in Leviticus belong to the "Holiness Code," which is the heart of the book and which challenges the people of God to follow his laws and not copy the practices either of Egypt (where they used to live) or of Canaan (to which he was bringing them). These practices included sexual relations within the prohibited degrees, a variety of sexual deviations, child sacrifice, idolatry and social injustice of different kinds. In this context we must read the following:

Do not lie with a man as one lies with a woman; that is detestable. (18:22)

If a man lies with a man as one lies with a woman, both of them have done what is detestable. They must be put to death; their blood will be on their own heads. (20:13)

"It is hardly open to doubt," wrote Bailey, "that both the laws in Leviticus relate to ordinary homosexual acts between men, and not to ritual or other acts performed in the name of religion."[9] Others, however, affirm the very point which Bailey denies. They rightly point out that the two texts are embedded in a context preoccupied largely with ritual cleanness, and Peter Coleman adds that the word translated "detestable" or "abomination" in both verses is associated with idolatry. "In English the word expresses disgust or disapproval, but in the Bible its predominant meaning is concerned with religious truth rather than morality or aesthetics."[10]

Are these prohibitions merely religious taboos, then? Are they connected with that other prohibition "no Israelite man or woman is to become a temple prostitute". (Deut 23:17)? Certainly the Canaanitish fertility cult did include ritual prostitution (even if there is no clear evidence that the male and female prostitutes engaged in homosexual intercourse). The evil kings of Israel and Judah were constantly introducing them into the religion of Yahweh, and the righteous kings were constantly expelling them.[11] The homosexual lobby argues therefore that the Levitical texts prohibit religious practices which have long since ceased, and have no relevance to homosexual partnerships today.

3. *Paul's Statements in Romans 1,* "Because of this, God gave them over to shameful lusts. Even their women exchanged natural relations for unnatural ones. In the same way the men also abandoned natural relations with women and were inflamed with lust for one another. Men committed indecent acts with other men, and received in themselves the due penalty for their perversion" (vv. 26-27).

All agree that the apostle is describing idolatrous pagans in the Greco-Roman world of his day. It seems at first sight to be a definite condemnation of homosexual behavior. But two arguments are advanced on the other side: (1) although Paul knew nothing of the modern distinction between "inverts" (who have a homosexual disposition) and "perverts" (who, though heterosexually inclined, indulge in homosexual practices), nevertheless it is the latter he is condemning, not the former. This must be so, because they are described as having "abandoned" natural relations with women, whereas no exclusively homosexual male would ever have had them. (2) Paul is evidently portraying the reckless, shameless, profligate, promiscuous behavior of people whom God has judicially "given up"; what relevance has this to committed, loving homosexual partnerships?

4. *The Other Pauline Texts.* In 1 Corinthians and 1 Timothy, Paul provides a list of sinners that include references to homosexual practices of some kind:

> Do you not know that the wicked will not inherit the kingdom of God? Do not be deceived: Neither the sexually immoral nor idolaters nor adulterers nor male prostitutes *[malakoi]* nor homosexual offenders *[arsenokoitai]* nor thieves nor the greedy nor drunkards nor slanderers nor swindlers will inherit the kingdom of God. (1 Cor 6:9-10)

> We also know that law is made not for righteous but for lawbreakers and rebels, the ungodly and sinful, the unholy and irreligious; for those who kill their fathers or mothers, for murderers, for adulterers and perverts *[arsenokoitai]*, for slave traders and liars and perjurers—and for whatever else is contrary to the sound doctrine that conforms to the glorious gospel of the blessed God. (1 Tim 1:9-10)

Here are two ugly lists of sins which Paul affirms to be incompatible in the first place with the kingdom of God and in the second with either the law or the gospel. One group of offenders is called *malakoi* and another (in both lists) *arsenokoitai*. What do these words mean?

The two Greek words *malakoi* and *arsenokoitai* should not be combined,[12] since they "have precise meanings. The first is literally 'soft to the touch' and metaphorically, among the Greeks, meant males (not necessarily boys) who played the passive role in homosexual intercourse. The second means literally 'male in a bed' and the Greeks used this expression to describe the one who took the active role."[13] Peter Coleman suggests that "probably Paul had commercial pederasty in mind between older men and postpubertal boys, the most common pattern of homosexual behaviour in the classical world."[14] If this is so, then once again it can be argued that the Pauline condemnations are not relevant to homosexual adults who are both consenting and committed to one another. Not that this is the conclusion which Peter Coleman himself draws: "Taken together, St. Paul's writings repudiate homosexual behaviour as a vice of the Gentiles in Romans, as a bar to the Kingdom in Corinthians, and as an offence to be repudiated by the moral law in 1 Timothy."[15]

Because there are only these four biblical references to homosexual behavior, must we then conclude that the topic is marginal to the main thrust of the Bible? Must we further concede that they constitute a rather flimsy basis on which to take a firm stand against a homosexual lifestyle? Are those protagonists right who claim that the biblical prohibitions are "highly specific"[16]—against violations of hospitality (Sodom and Gibeah), against cultic taboos (Leviticus), against shameless orgies (Romans) and against male prostitution or the corruption of the young (1 Corinthians and 1 Timothy), and that none of these passages alludes to, let alone condemns, a loving partnership between genuine homosexual inverts? This is the conclusion reached, for example, by Letha Scanzoni and Virginia Mollenkott in their book *Is the Homosexual My Neighbor?* They write:

> The Bible clearly condemns certain kinds of homosexual practice (. . . gang rape, idolatry, and lustful promiscuity). However, it appears to be silent on certain other aspects of homosexuality—both the "homosexual orientation" and "a committed love-relationship analogous to heterosexual monogamy."[17]

But we cannot handle the biblical material in this way. The Christian rejection of homosexual practices does not rest on "a few isolated and obscure proof texts" (as is sometimes said), whose traditional explanation can be overthrown. And it is disturbing to me that those who write on this subject, and include in their treatment a section on the biblical teaching, all seem to deal with it in this way. For example, "Consideration of the Christian attitude to homosexual practices," wrote Sherwin Bailey, "inevitably begins with the story of the destruction of Sodom and Gomorrah."[18] But this beginning is not at all "inevitable." In fact, it is positively mistaken, for the *negative* prohibitions of homosexual practices in Scripture make sense only in the light of its *positive* teaching in Genesis 1 and 2 about human sexuality and heterosexual marriage. Without the teaching of the Bible on sex and marriage, our perspective on the homosexual question is bound to be skewed.

Sex and Marriage in the Bible
Since gay Christian activists deliberately draw a parallel

between heterosexual marriages and homosexual partnerships, it is necessary to ask whether this parallel can be justified.

God has given us two distinct accounts of creation. The first (Gen 1) is general and affirms the *equality* of the sexes, since both share in the image of God and the stewardship of the earth. The second (Gen 2) is particular and affirms the *complementarity* of the sexes, which constitutes the basis for heterosexual marriage. In this second account three fundamental truths emerge.

First, *the human need for companionship.* "It is not good for the man to be alone" (2:18). God has created us social beings. Since he is love and has made us in his own likeness, he has given us a capacity to love and to be loved. He intends us to live in community, not in solitude. In particular, God continued, "I will make a helper suitable for him." Moreover, this "helper" or companion, whom God pronounced "suitable for him," was also to be his sexual partner, with whom he was to become "one flesh," so that they might thereby both consummate their love and procreate their children. (Paul later qualifies this statement in 1 Corinthians 7 by teaching that the call to singleness is also the good vocation of some.)

Second, Genesis 2 reveals *the divine provision to meet this human need.* Having affirmed Adam's need for a partner, the search for a suitable one began. God first paraded the birds and beasts before him, and Adam proceeded to "name" them, to symbolize his taking them into his service. But "for Adam no suitable helper was found" who could live "alongside" or "opposite" him, who could be his complement, his counterpart, his companion, let alone his mate (v. 20). So a special creation was necessary.

Thus a special work of divine creation took place. The sexes became differentiated. Out of the undifferentiated humanity of Adam, male and female emerged. Adam awoke from his deep sleep to behold a reflection of himself, a complement to himself, indeed a very part of himself. Next, having created the woman out of the man, God himself brought her to him, much as today the bride's father gives the bride away. And Adam broke spontaneously into history's first love poem:

This at last [in contrast to the birds and beasts]

is bone of my bones

and flesh of my flesh;

she shall be called Woman,

because she was taken out of Man. (2:23 RSV)

There can be no doubting the emphasis of this story. According to Genesis 1, Eve like Adam was created in the image of God. But as to the manner of her creation, according to Genesis 2, she was made neither out of nothing (like the universe), nor out of "the dust of the ground" (like Adam), but out of Adam.

The third great truth of Genesis 2 concerns *the resulting institution of marriage*. Adam's love poem is recorded in verse 23. Verse 24 contains the narrator's deduction: "For this reason a man will leave his father and mother and be united to his wife, and they will become one flesh."

Even the inattentive reader will be struck by the three references to "flesh": "this is . . . *flesh* of my *flesh*. . . . They will become one *flesh.*" We may be certain that this is deliberate, not accidental. It teaches that heterosexual intercourse in marriage is more than a union; it is a kind of reunion. It is not a union of alien persons who do not belong to one another and cannot appropriately become one flesh. On the contrary, it is the union of two persons who originally were one, were then separated from each other, and now in the sexual encounter of marriage come together again.

It is surely this which explains the profound mystery of heterosexual intimacy, which poets and philosophers have celebrated in every culture. Heterosexual intercourse is much more than a union of bodies; it is a blending of complementary personalities through which, in the midst of prevailing alienation, the rich created oneness of human being is experienced again. And the complementarity of male and female sexual organs is only a symbol at the physical level of a much deeper spiritual complementarity.

To become one flesh, however, and experience this sacred mystery, we see from verse 24 that certain preliminaries are necessary, which are constituent parts of marriage. "For this reason *a man*" (the singular indicates that marriage is an exclusive union between two individuals) *"will leave his father and mother"* (a public social occasion is in view) *"and be united to his wife"* (marriage is a loving, cleaving commitment or covenant, which is heterosexual and permanent) *"and they will become one flesh"* (for marriage must be consummated in sexual intercourse, which is a sign and seal of the marriage covenant, and over which no shadow of shame or embarrassment had yet been cast [see v. 25]).

Jesus himself later endorsed this teaching. He quoted Genesis 2:24, declared that such a lifelong union between a man and his wife was God's intention from the beginning, and added "what God has joined together, let man not separate" (Mk 10:4-9).

Thus Scripture defines marriage in terms of heterosexual monogamy. It is the union of one man with one woman, which must be publicly acknowledged (the leaving of parents), permanently sealed (he will "cleave to his wife") and physically consummated ("one flesh"). And Scripture envisages no other kind of marriage or sexual intercourse, for God provided no alternative.

Christians should not therefore single out homosexual intercourse for special condemnation. The fact is that every sexual relationship or act which deviates from God's revealed intention is *ipso facto* displeasing to him and under his judgment. This includes polygamy and polyandry (which infringe the "one man-one woman" principle), clandestine unions (since these have involved no decisive public leaving of parents), casual encounters and temporary liaisons, adultery and many divorces (which are incompatible with "cleaving" and with Jesus' prohibition "let man not separate"), and homosexual partnerships (which violate the statement that "a man" shall be joined to "his wife").

In sum, the only "one flesh" experience which God intends and Scripture contemplates is the sexual union of a man with his wife, whom he recognizes as "flesh of his flesh."

Contemporary Arguments Considered

Homosexual Christians are not, however, satisfied with this biblical teaching about human sexuality and the institution of heterosexual marriage. They bring forward a number of objections in order to defend the legitimacy of homosexual partnerships.

1. *The argument about Scripture and culture.* Traditionally, it has been assumed that the Bible condemns all homosexual acts. But are the biblical writers reliable guides in this matter? Were their horizons not bounded by their own experience and culture? The cultural argument usually takes one of two forms.

First, the biblical authors were addressing themselves to questions relevant to their own circumstances, and these were very different from ours. In the Sodom and Gibeah stories they were preoccupied either with conventions of hospitality in the Ancient Near East which are now obsolete or (if the sin was sexual at all) with the extremely unusual phenomenon of homosexual gang rape. In the Levitical laws the concern was with antiquated fertility rituals, while Paul was addressing himself to the particular sexual preferences of Greek pederasts. It is all so antiquarian. The biblical authors' imprisonment in their own cultures renders their teaching on this topic irrelevant.

The second and complementary problem is that these writers were not addressing themselves to our questions. Paul and the Old Testament authors had never heard of "the homosexual condition" of post-Freudian psychology; they knew only about certain practices. The difference between "inversion" and "perversion" would have been incomprehensible to them. The very notion that two men or two women could fall in love and develop a deeply loving, stable relationship comparable to marriage simply never entered their heads. So then, just as slaves, blacks and women have been liberated, "gay liberation" is long overdue.

If the only biblical teaching on this topic were to be found in the prohibition texts, it might be difficult to answer these objections. But once those texts are seen in relation to the divine institution of marriage, we are in possession of a principle of divine revelation which is universally applicable. It was applicable to the cultural situations of both the Ancient Near East and the first-century Greco-Roman world, and it is equally applicable to modern sexual questions of which the ancients were quite ignorant. The reason for the prohibitions is the same reason why loving homosexual partnerships must also be condemned, namely, that they are incompatible with God's created order. And since that order (heterosexual monogamy) was established by creation, not culture, its validity is both permanent and universal. There can be no "liberation" from God's created norms; true liberation is found only in accepting them.

2. *The argument about creation and nature.* I have sometimes read or heard this kind of statement: "I'm gay because God made me that way. So gay must be good." Norman Pittenger was quite outspoken in his use of this argument a couple of decades ago. A homosexual person, he wrote, is "not an 'abnormal' person with 'unnatural' desires and habits." On the contrary, "a heterosexually oriented person acts 'naturally' when he acts heterosexually, while a homosexually oriented person acts equally 'naturally' when he acts in accordance with his basic, inbuilt homosexual desire and drive."[19] Others argue that homosexual behavior is "natural" (a) because in many primitive societies it is fairly acceptable, (b) because in some advanced civilizations (ancient Greece, for example) it was even idealized, and (c) because it is quite widespread in animals.

But these arguments express an extremely subjective view of what is "natural" and "normal." We should not accept Pittenger's statement that there are "no external standards of normality or naturalness."[20] Nor can we agree that animal behavior sets standards for human behavior! God has established a norm for sex and marriage by creation. This was already recognized in the Old Testament era. Thus sexual relations with an animal were forbidden because "that is a perversion" (Lev 18:23)—in other words, a violation or confusion of nature, which indicates an "embryonic sense of natural law."[21]

The same concept was clearly in Paul's mind in Romans 1. When he wrote of women who had "exchanged natural relations for unnatural ones," and of men who had "abandoned natural relations," he meant by "nature" *(phusis)* the natural order of things which God has established (as in 2:14, 27 and 11:24). What Paul was condemning, therefore, was not the perverted behavior of heterosexual people who were acting against their nature, but any human behavior which is against "Nature," that is, against God's created order.

3. *The argument about quality of relationships.* The Gay Christian Movement borrows from Scripture the truth that love is the greatest thing in the world (which it is) and from the "new morality" or "situation ethics" of the 1960s the notion that love is an adequate criterion by which to judge every relationship (which it is not). This view is gaining ground today.

In his *Time for Consent* Norman Pittenger lists six characteristics of a truly loving relationship. They are (1) commitment, (2) mutuality in giving and receiving, (3) tenderness (no coercion or cruelty), (4) faithfulness (the intention of a lifelong relationship), (5) hopefulness (each serving the other's maturity) and (6) desire for union.[22]

If then a homosexual relationship, whether between two men or two women, is characterized by these qualities of love, surely (the argument runs) it must be affirmed as good and not rejected as evil. It rescues people from loneliness, selfishness and promiscuity. It can be just as rich and responsible, as liberating and fulfilling, as a heterosexual marriage.

But the biblical Christian cannot accept the basic

premise on which this case rests, namely, that love is the only absolute, that beside it all moral law has been abolished, and that whatever seems to be compatible with love is *ipso facto* good, irrespective of all other considerations. This cannot be so. For love needs law to guide it. In emphasizing love for God and neighbor as the two great commandments, Jesus and his apostles did not discard all other commandments. On the contrary, Jesus said "if you love me you will keep my commandments" (Jn 14:15) and Paul wrote "love is the fulfilling [not the abrogating] of the law" (Rom 13:8-10).

On several different occasions a married man has told me that he has fallen in love with another woman. When I have reminded him that he already has a wife and family, he has responded in words like these: "But this new relationship is the real thing. We were made for each other. Our love for each other has a quality and depth we have never known before. It must be right." But no, I have had to say, it is not right. No man is justified in breaking his marriage covenant on the ground of the quality of his love for another woman. Quality of love is not the only yardstick by which to measure what is good or right.

Similarly, I do not deny the claim that homosexual relationships can be loving (although *a priori* I do not see how they can attain the same richness as the heterosexual mutuality God has ordained). But their love-quality is not sufficient to justify them. Indeed, I have to add that they are incompatible with true love because they are incompatible with God's law. Love is concerned for the highest welfare of the beloved. And our highest human welfare is found in obedience to God's law and purpose, not in revolt against them.

4. *The argument about acceptance and the gospel.* Some

argue that it is our duty to accept homosexual Christians. If God has welcomed somebody, who are we to pass judgment on him (Rom 14:1-4)? Pittenger goes further and declares that those who reject homosexual people "have utterly failed to understand the Christian gospel." We do not receive the grace of God because we are good and confess our sins; it is the other way around. He even quotes the hymn "Just As I Am, Without One Plea," and adds: "The whole point of the Christian gospel is that God loves and accepts us just as we are."[23]

This is a very confused statement of the gospel, however. God does indeed accept us "just as we are," and we do not have to make ourselves good first—indeed we cannot. But his acceptance means that he fully and freely forgives all who repent and believe, not that he condones our continuance in sin. Again, it is true that we must accept one another, but only as fellow penitents and fellow pilgrims, not as fellow sinners who are resolved to persist in our sinning. No acceptance, either by God or by the church, is promised to us if we harden our hearts against God's Word and will—only judgment.

Faith, Hope and Love
If homosexual practice must be regarded not as a variant within the wide range of accepted normality, but as a deviation from God's norm; and if we should therefore call homosexually oriented people to abstain from homosexual practices and partnerships, what advice and help can we give to encourage them to respond to this call? I would like to take Paul's triad of faith, hope and love, and apply it to homosexually oriented people.

The Christian call to faith. Faith is the human response to divine revelation; it is believing God's Word.

First, *faith accepts God's standards*. The only alternative to heterosexual marriage is sexual abstinence. I think I know the implications of this. Nothing has helped me to understand the pain of homosexual celibacy more than Alex Davidson's moving book *The Returns of Love.* He writes of "this incessant tension between law and lust," "this monster that lurks in the depths," this "burning torment."[24]

The secular world says: "Sex is essential to human fulfillment. To expect homosexual people to abstain from homosexual practice is to condemn them to frustration and to drive them to neurosis, despair and even suicide. It's 'inhuman and inhumane'[25] to ask anybody to deny himself what to him is a normal and natural mode of sexual expression. Indeed, it's positively cruel."

But no, the Word of God teaches that sexual experience is not essential to human fulfillment. To be sure, it is a good gift of God. But it is not given to all, and it is not indispensable to humanness. Jesus Christ was single, yet perfect in his humanity. God's commands are good and not grievous. The yoke of Christ brings rest not turmoil; conflict comes only to those who resist it.

So ultimately it is a crisis of faith: Whom shall we believe? God or the world? Shall we submit to the lordship of Jesus, or succumb to the pressures of prevailing culture? The true "orientation" of Christians is not what we are by constitution, but what we are by choice.

Second, *faith accepts God's grace*. Abstinence is not only good if God calls us to celibacy; it is also possible. Many deny it, however. To control our sex drive is "so near to an impossibility," writes Norman Pittenger, "that it's hardly worth talking about."[26]

Really? What then are we to make of Paul's statement following his warning to the Corinthians that male prostitutes and homosexual offenders will not inherit God's kingdom? "And that is what some of you were," he cries. "But you were washed, you were sanctified, you were justified in the name of the Lord Jesus Christ and by the Spirit of our God" (1 Cor 6:11). And what shall we say· to the millions of heterosexual people who are single? To be sure, all unmarried people experience the pain of struggle and loneliness. But how can we call ourselves Christians and declare that chastity is impossible? It is made harder by the sexual obsession of contemporary society. And we make it harder for ourselves if we listen to the world's plausible arguments, or lapse into self-pity, or feed our imagination with pornographic material and so inhabit a fantasy world in which Christ is not Lord, or ignore his command about being ruthless with the avenues of temptation (Mt 5:29-30). But, whatever our "thorn in the flesh" may be, Christ comes to us as he came to Paul and says: "My grace is sufficient for you, for my power is made perfect in weakness" (2 Cor 12:9). To deny this is to portray Christians as the helpless victims of the world, the flesh and the devil, and to contradict the gospel of God's grace.

The Christian call to hope. I have said nothing so far about the "healing" of homosexual people, understood now not as self-mastery but as the reversal of their sexual bias. Our expectation of this possibility will depend largely on our understanding of the etiology of the homosexual condition. Dr. West writes, "Research into the causes of homosexuality has left a lot of mysteries unsolved."[27] In his view, however, "children are not born with the sex instinct specifically directed to one sex or the other. Exclusive preference for the opposite sex is an acquired trait."[28] So, if it is learned, can it not be unlearned?

Those whose sexuality is indeterminate may well change under strong influence and with strong motivation. But many researchers conclude that constitutional homosexuality is irreversible. "No known method of treatment or punishment," writes West, "offers hope of making any substantial reduction in the vast army of adults practising homosexuality." He pleads for "tolerance," though not for "encouragement" of homosexual behavior.[29] Other psychologists go further and declare that homosexuality is no longer to be regarded as a pathological condition; it is therefore to be accepted, not cured. In 1973 the trustees of the American Psychiatric Association removed homosexuality from the category of mental illness.

Are not these views, however, the despairing opinions of the secular mind? Christians know that the homosexual condition, being a deviation from God's norm, is not a sign of created order but of fallen disorder. How, then, can we acquiesce in it or declare it incurable?

We cannot. The only question is *when* and *how* we are to expect the divine deliverance and restoration to take place. The fact is that, though Christian claims of homosexual "healings" are made, it is not easy to substantiate them. Martin Hallett, who before his conversion was active in the gay scene, has subsequently founded the True Freedom Trust, an interdenominational teaching and counseling ministry on homosexuality and related problems.[30] They have published a pamphlet entitled *Testimonies*. In it homosexual Christian men and women bear witness to what Christ has done for them. They have found a new identity in him, and a new sense of personal fulfillment as children of God. They have been delivered from guilt, shame and fear by God's forgiving acceptance, and set free from thralldom to their former homosexual activity by the indwelling power of the Holy Spirit. But they are not delivered from their homosexual orientation, and therefore some inner pain continues alongside their new joy and peace.

But what are the prospects of a substantial change of orientation? Dr. Elizabeth Moberly has been led by her research to the view that "a homosexual orientation does not depend on genetic predisposition, hormonal imbalance, or abnormal learning processes, but on difficulties in the parent-child relationship, especially in the earlier years of life." The "underlying principle," she continues, is "that the homosexual—whether man or woman—has suffered from some deficit in the relationship with the parent *of the same sex;* and that there is a corresponding drive to make good this deficit through the medium of same-sex or 'homosexual' relationships."[31] The deficit and the drive go together. The reparative drive for same-sex love is not itself pathological, but "quite the opposite—it is the attempt to resolve and heal the pathology." "The homosexual condition does not involve abnormal needs, but normal needs that have, abnormally, been left unmet in the ordinary process of growth." Homosexuality "is essentially a state of incomplete development" or of unmet needs.[32] So the proper solution is "the meeting of same-sex needs without sexual activity," for to eroticize growth deficits is to confuse emotional needs with physiological desires.[33]

How, then, can these needs be met? Dr. Moberly's answer is that "substitute relationships for parental care are in God's redemptive plan, just as parental relationships are in his creative plan."[34] What is needed is deep, loving, lasting, same-sex but nonsexual relationships, especially in the church. "Love," she concludes, "both in prayer and in relationships, is the best therapy. . . .

Love is the basic problem, the great need, and the only true solution. If we are willing to seek and to mediate the healing and redeeming love of Christ, then healing for the homosexual will become a great and glorious reality."[35]

Even then, however, complete healing will not take place in this life. Some degree of deficit or disorder remains in each of us. But not forever! Jesus is coming again; our bodies are going to be redeemed; sin, pain and death are going to be abolished; and both we and the universe are going to be transformed. Then we shall be finally liberated from everything which defiles or distorts our personality. This Christian assurance helps us to bear whatever our present pain may be, for pain there is, in the midst of peace. "The whole creation has been groaning as in the pains of childbirth right up to the present time. Not only so, but we ourselves, who have the firstfruits of the Spirit, groan inwardly as we wait eagerly for our adoption as sons, the redemption of our bodies" (Rom 8:22-23). Thus our groans express the birth pangs of the new age. We are convinced that "our present sufferings are not worth comparing with the glory that will be revealed in us" (Rom 8:18). This confident hope sustains us.

In the midst of his homosexuality Alex Davidson derives comfort from his Christian hope. "Isn't it one of the most wretched things about this condition," he writes, "that when you look ahead, the same impossible road seems to continue indefinitely? You're driven to rebellion when you think of there being no point in it, and to despair when you think of there being no limit to it. That's why I find a comfort, when I feel desperate, or rebellious, or both, to remind myself of God's promise that one day it will be finished."[36]

The Christian call to love. At present we are living "in between times," between the grace which we grasp by faith and the glory which we anticipate in hope. Between them lies love.

Yet love is just what the church has generally failed to show to homosexual people. Jim Cotter complains bitterly about being treated as "objects of scorn and insult, of fear, prejudice and oppression."[37] Norman Pittenger describes the "vituperative" correspondence he has received, in which homosexuals are dismissed even by professing Christians as "filthy creatures," "disgusting perverts," "damnable sinners," and the like.[38] Pierre Berton, a social commentator, writes that "a very good case can be made out that the homosexual is the modern equivalent of the leper."[39] Rictor Norton is yet more shrill: "The church's record regarding homosexuals is an atrocity from beginning to end: it is not for us to seek forgiveness, but for the church to make atonement."[40]

The attitude of personal hostility toward homosexuals is nowadays termed "homophobia."[41] It is a mixture of irrational fear, hatred and even revulsion. It overlooks the fact that the great majority of homosexual people are not responsible for their condition (though they are, of course, for their conduct). Since they are not deliberate perverts, they deserve our understanding and compassion (though many find this patronizing), not our rejection. No wonder Richard Lovelace calls for "a double repentance," namely, "that gay Christians renounce the active lifestyle" and that "straight Christians renounce homophobia."[42] David Atkinson is right to add: "We are not at liberty to urge the Christian homosexual to celibacy and to a spreading of his relationships, unless support for the former and opportunities for the latter are available in genuine love."[43] I rather think that the very existence of the Gay Christian Movement, not to mention the so-called Evangelical Fellowship within it, is a vote of censure on the church.

At the heart of the homosexual condition is a deep loneliness, the natural human hunger for mutual love, a search for identity and a longing for completeness. If homosexual people cannot find these things in the local "church family," we have no business to go on using that expression. The alternative is not between the warm physical relationship of homosexual intercourse and the pain of isolation in the cold. There is a third alternative, namely, a Christian environment of love, understanding, acceptance and support. I do not think there is any need to encourage homosexual people to disclose their sexual orientation to everybody; this is neither necessary nor helpful. But they do need at least one confidant to whom they can unburden themselves, who will not despise or reject them, but will support them with friendship and prayer; probably some professional, private and confidential pastoral counsel; possibly in addition the support of a professionally supervised therapy group; and many warm and affectionate friendships with people of both sexes. Same-sex friendships are to be encouraged, like those in the Bible between Ruth and Naomi, David and Jonathan, and Paul and Timothy. There is no hint that any of these were homosexual in the erotic sense, yet they were evidently affectionate and (at least in the case of David and Jonathan) even demonstrative.[44] Of course sensible safeguards will be important. But in African and Asian cultures it is common to see two men walking down the street hand in hand, without embarrassment. It is sad that our Western culture inhibits the development of rich same-sex friendships by engendering the fear of being ridiculed or rejected as a "queer."

These relationships, both same-sex and opposite-sex, need to be developed within the family of God which, though universal, has its local manifestations. He intends each local church to be a warm, accepting and supportive community. By "accepting" I do not mean "acquiescing," any more than in rejecting homophobia I am rejecting a proper Christian disapproval of homosexual behavior. No, true love is not incompatible with the maintenance of moral standards. There is, therefore, a place for church discipline in the case of members who refuse to repent and willfully persist in homosexual relationships. But it must be exercised in a spirit of humility and gentleness (Gal 6:1-2); we must be careful not to discriminate between men and women, or between homosexual and heterosexual offenses; and necessary discipline in the case of a public scandal is not to be confused with a witch-hunt.

Perplexing and painful as the homosexual Christian's dilemma is, Jesus Christ offers him or her (indeed, all of us) faith, hope and love—the faith to accept his standards, and his grace to maintain them, the hope to look beyond present suffering to future glory, and the love to care for and support one another. "But the greatest of these is love" (1 Cor 13:13).

Notes

[1] See A. C. Kinsey's *Sexual Behavior in the Human Male* (1948) and *Sexual Behavior in the Human Female* (1953). His research methods and findings have been criticized, however; the former for being selective and the latter in consequence for showing a misleadingly high percentage of abnormality.

[2] Donald J. West, *Homosexuality*, 3rd ed. (Eng.: Duckworth, 1968), p. 12.

[3] From an article entitled, "God, Sex and You," *Eternity* magazine, August 1972.

[4] J. N. D. Anderson, *Morality, Law and Grace* (Downers Grove, Ill.: InterVarsity Press, 1972), p. 73.

[5] Malcolm Macourt, ed., *Towards a Theology of Gay Liberation* (London: SCM Press, 1977), p. 3. The quotation comes from Macourt's own introduction to the book.

[6] Derrick Sherwin Bailey, *Homosexuality and the Western Christian Tradition* (Harlow, Eng.: Longmans, Green, 1955), p. 4.

[7] Bailey gives references in the *Book of Jubilees* and the *Testaments of the Twelve Patriarchs* (ibid., pp. 11-20). There is an even fuller evaluation of the writings of the intertestamental period in Peter Coleman, *Christian Attitudes to Homosexuality* (London: SPCK, 1980), pp. 58-85.

[8] James D. Martin in *Towards a Theology of Gay Liberation*, p. 53.

[9] Bailey, *Homosexuality and the Western Christian Tradition*, p. 30.

[10] Coleman, *Christian Attitudes to Homosexuality*, p. 49.

[11] See, for example, 1 Kings 14:22-24; 15:12; 22:46 and 2 Kings 23:7.

[12] In the original Revised Standard Version translation of 1 Corinthians 6:9, the words were combined and translated as "homosexuals." Though later revised (1973), Bailey was right to protest, since the use of the word *homosexuals* "inevitably suggests that the genuine invert, even though he be a man of irreproachable morals, is automatically branded as unrighteous and excluded from the kingdom of God" (Bailey, *Homosexuality and the Western Christian Tradition*, p. 39).

[13] Coleman, *Christian Attitudes to Homosexuality*, pp. 95-96.

[14] Ibid., p. 277.

[15] Ibid., p. 101.

[16]Rictor Norton in *Towards a Theology of Gay Liberation*, p. 58.

[17]Letha Scanzoni and Virginia R. Mollencott, *Is the Homosexual My Neighbor?* (San Francisco: Harper & Row, 1978), p. 111.

[18]Bailey, *Homosexuality and the Western Christian Tradition*, p. 1.

[19]Norman Pittenger, *Time for Consent*, 3rd ed. (London: SCM, 1976), pp. 7, 73.

[20]Ibid., p. 7.

[21]Coleman, *Christian Attitudes to Homosexuality*, p. 50.

[22]Pittenger, *Time for Consent*, pp. 30-31.

[23]Ibid., p. 94.

[24]Alex Davidson, *The Returns of Love* (Downers Grove, Ill.: InterVarsity Press, 1970), pp. 12, 16, 49.

[25]Norman Pittenger in *Towards a Theology of Gay Liberation*, p. 87.

[26]Pittenger, *Time for Consent*, p. 7.

[27]West, *Homosexuality*, p. 261.

[28]Ibid., p. 15. Professor R. J. Berry provides a useful summary of current opinion on etiology in his contribution to the 1982 London Lectures, *Free to be Different* (Basingstoke, Eng.: Marshalls, 1984), pp. 108-16.

[29]West, *Homosexuality*, pp. 266, 273.

[30]The address of the True Freedom Trust is P.O. Box 3, Upton, Wirral, Merseyside L49 6NY, England.

[31]Elizabeth R. Moberly, *Homosexuality: A New Christian Ethic* (Cambridge, Eng.: James Clarke, 1983), p. 2.

[32]Ibid. p. 28.

[33]Ibid., pp. 18-20.

[34]Ibid., pp. 35-36.

[35]Ibid., p. 52.

[36]Davidson, *The Returns of Love*, p. 51.

[37]Jim Cotter in *Towards a Theology of Gay Liberation*, p. 63.

[38]Pittenger, *Time for Consent*, p. 2.

[39]Letha Scanzoni and Virginia R. Mollencott quoted in *The Comfortable Pew* (1965).

[40]Rictor Norton in *Towards a Theology of Gay Liberation*, p. 45.

[41]The word seems to have been used first by George Weinberg in *Society and the Healthy Homosexual* (New York: Doubleday, 1973).

[42]Richard F. Lovelace, *Homosexuality and the Church* (Old Tappan, N.J.: Revell, 1978), p. 129; see also p. 125.

[43]David J. Atkinson, *Homosexuals in the Christian Fellowship* (Oxford: Latimer House, 1979), p. 118.

[44]See 1 Samuel 20:41 and 2 Samuel 1:26.